The Cabots and the discovery of America: with a description and history of Brandon Hill, the site of the Cabot Memorial Tower

Hodges

1	2	3

1
2
3

1	2	3
4	5	6

The Cabots
and the
Discovery
of America.

* * * *

By
Elizabeth Hodges.

Illustrated by
S. Loxton.

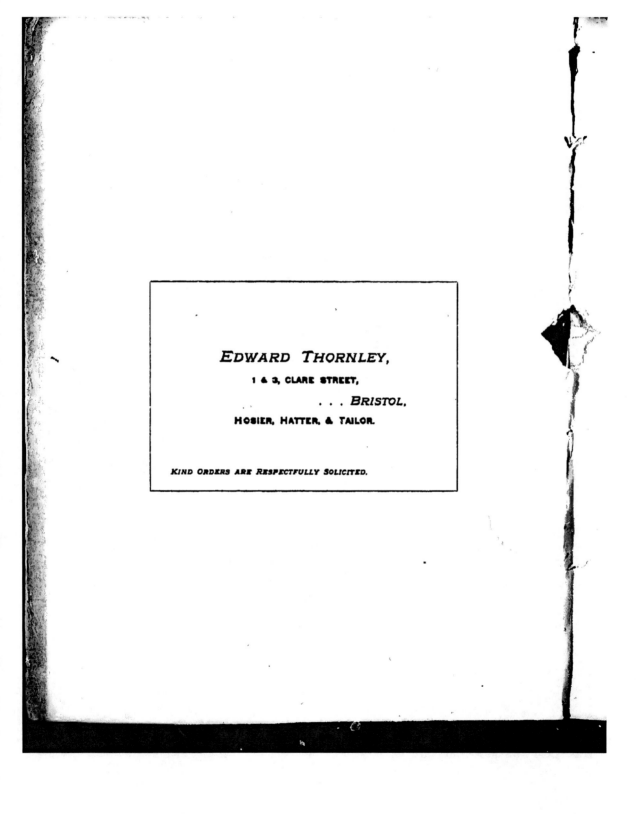

EDWARD THORNLEY,

1 & 3, CLARE STREET,

. . . BRISTOL,

HOSIER, HATTER, & TAILOR.

KIND ORDERS ARE RESPECTFULLY SOLICITED.

The Cabots

and the

Discovery of America.

WITH A

BRIEF DESCRIPTION AND HISTORY

OF BRANDON HILL, THE SITE

OF THE

CABOT MEMORIAL TOWER.

By ELIZABETH HODGES.

Illustrated by S. LOXTON.

London:

ERNEST NISTER, 28, PATERNOSTER ROW.

Bristol:

W. F. MACK & CO., 52, PARK ROW.

And of all Booksellers.

Bristol :
W. F. Mack & Co.,
Crown Printing Works,
52, Park Row.

TO THE RIGHT HON. THE

MARQUESS OF DUFFERIN & AVA,

K.P., G.C.B., F.R.S., etc.,

WHOSE ADMINISTRATION FROM 1872 TO 1878

AS GOVERNOR-GENERAL OF

THE LAND DISCOVERED BY THE CABOTS

WILL EVER RANK AMONGST THE HIGHEST,

THIS BROCHURE IS,

BY HIS KIND PERMISSION,

RESPECTFULLY DEDICATED.

Cabot Memorial Tower.

WM. V. GOUGH, ARCHITECT.   LOVE & WAITE, BUILDERS.

and the

Discovery of America.

By ELIZABETH HODGES.

CHIEF among the attractions of Bristol has been
for centuries past the church of St. Mary
Redcliffe; while few names on her roll of fame are
more widely known than that of the ancient citizen
to whom the stately fabric owes so much of its grace
and beauty.

And we grudge not the mead of praise. He who
gives of his best to the service of God and his fellow
men deserves high honour. But, when all is said, the
work of William Canynge was as a drop in the ocean
compared with that accomplished by the merchant-
pilot, his contemporary and probable neighbour.
Canynge helped to re-build a church; John Cabot
discovered a continent, and secured it for all time to
the English-speaking race. Yet the one has been
remembered and revered; the other neglected and
forgotten. An anomaly, perhaps accounted for by the

fact that Bristol has ever been slow to recognise merit outside her borders, and John Cabot was an alien, while the claims of Sebastian, his son, to citizenship are still hotly contested; which is not surprising, as the evidence so far obtainable rests mainly upon the contradictory accounts of Sebastian himself.

To an unprejudiced mind, however, the assertion made by him to his friend Eden in old age, when he had no purpose in view and nothing to gain by it, "that he was borne in Bristowe, and at iiii. yeare ould he was carried with his father to Venice, and so returned agayne to England with his father after

St. Mary Redcliffe Church.

certayne years, whereby he was thought to have been borne in Venice," appears far more likely to be true than his statement in middle life to Contarini, the Venetian Ambassador, by which he sought to obtain

of little moment, even to Bristolians; nor the question
of earlier voyages, so long as the great fact remains—
That it was from Bristol port, in a Bristol ship,

St. Augustine's Bridge at head of the Quay.

manned by Bristol sailors, on the initiative of Bristol
merchants, that John Cabot sailed on that memorable
May morning four hundred years ago; and that to

eastern-most point of Cape Breton, in the Dominion of
Canada, and taken possession of that great northern
continent for the King of England !—An achievement,
be it remembered, preceding by more than a year the

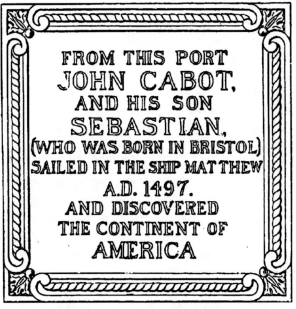

FROM THIS PORT
JOHN CABOT,
AND HIS SON
SEBASTIAN,
(WHO WAS BORN IN BRISTOL)
SAILED IN THE SHIP MATTHEW
A.D. 1497.
AND DISCOVERED
THE CONTINENT OF
AMERICA

Tablet on St. Augustine's Bridge.

landing of Columbus on the Southern continent.

That land across the wide Atlantic had been
discovered long before Cabot sighted it is now
generally admitted. Setting aside the claims of

Madoc the Welshman and the Irish sailor-saint Brendan as not yet proven, it is certain that the Icelanders planted a colony in Greenland as early as the tenth century. The colony perished, but its traditions remained and were the inciting cause of later voyages; for Bristol merchants trading with Iceland, heard thereof and sent out ships in search of the "new land" for seven successive years before the the sailing of the "Matthew"—thinking to get by way of it to the Indies, or "far Cathay," the name given to all countries east of the Persian Gulf.

Unfortunately for the future historian, Sebastian Cabot not only "romanced" concerning his birth-place, but also concerning his voyages; in consequence of which he has been, for centuries, honoured as the commander of the "Matthew" and the discoverer of America. Thanks, however, to modern research among musty rolls and ancient charters, it has been proved beyond a doubt that the commander of the Bristol ship and discoverer of the Continent was John Cabot. Whether Sebastian ever sailed at all on that first voyage is entirely conjectural. The evidence that he did rests mainly upon a reported conversation held with a stranger at Seville, in which he appears to have mixed up the discoveries of the first expedition with those of later ones, and ignoring his father's share, himself claimed credit for the whole!

A modern writer suggests in excuse that he feared to excite the jealous displeasure of the King of Spain, in whose service he then was, by attracting attention to the prior discovery of a continent which his Catholic majesty would fain claim as his own. Perhaps, however, as the conversation was transcribed not at second, but at third hand, the indictment may be best taken with the proverbial grain of salt; and, certainly, both on Sebastian's portrait and on his famous " Mappamundi," the claims of the elder Cabot are acknowledged.

Of John Cabot's birthplace no record exists, though some writers claim the honour for Bristol. Recent research, however, has proved him to have been of Norman extraction, descended from the Jersey Cabots or Chabots. In 1476, for purposes of commerce, he became a Venetian citizen. When he first came to London " to follow the trade of merchandise " is uncertain; but he ultimately found his way to Bristol, which he appears to have made his home for some years. As strangers were not allowed to remain within the city to trade longer than forty days, in all probability he resided with his Venetian wife, among others of her nation, in the eastern suburb (the north and west were occupied by Jews) near to St. Mary Redcliffe, where a district still bears the suggestive name of " Cathay."

An enterprising and wealthy merchant, Cabot was

those golden lands across the western ocean, whose existence mariners of all nations had so long suspected.

Among Bristol merchants, baffled in their own attempts to reach the goal, such a man was sure of

Ship of Cabot's Time.

meeting with not only sympathy, but ready co-operation. And in 1496 we find him obtaining from Henry VII. a charter, made out in the names of himself and his sons, Lewis, Sebastian, and Sanctus, empowering him and those associated with him to fit out sundry vessels to search for new lands, and take possession of them in the name of the King, he and his heirs to occupy such lands as Henry's vassals and trade therein.

The "Matthew," a small vessel, was accordingly fitted out, sixteen Bristol men and a Burgundian forming the crew, and in her Cabot set sail from the ancient port, May 2nd, 1497.

Voyaging nearly due west, he, to quote from the contemporary letter of Lorenzo Pasqualigo, "wandered about a long time, and at length hit land"—not Bonavista, Newfoundland, nor Cape Chidley, Labrador, whose shores are ice-bound at that season; but Cape Breton, the easternmost point of Nova Scotia;—"he coasted 300 leagues and landed; saw no human beings, but brought to the King certain snares which had been set to catch game, and a needle for making nets; he also found some felled trees, wherefore supposing there were inhabitants, he returned to his ship in alarm." Two islands were subsequently sighted (St. John's and Newfoundland), but shortness of provisions compelled Cabot to return homewards without landing.

And so, after an absence of three months, the little ship, having safely braved the perils of those unknown seas and inhospitable shores, sailed

"Up the Avon's gentle flood and under Clifton's height" to her old anchorage beside the Quay.

On the 10th of August, her captain was in London

Old Bristol
Bridge
in 1500.

S Loxton
1897

relating his discoveries to the King. Henry was so pleased with Cabot's success that he gave him a pension of £20 for life, and "£10 to him who found (first sighted) the new isle." Pasqualigo tells how he was styled the "Great Admiral," dressed in rich silks, and had vast honours paid him, the English running after him "like mad people."

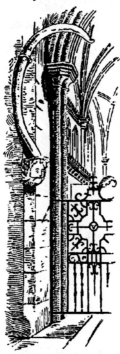

In these rejoicings Bristolians, we may be sure, took a prominent part, and many a city father and wealthy merchant, when office and shop were closed for the day, would wend his way across the ancient bridge and up Redcliffe Street to Cabot's home in "Cathay," to hear his stories of those distant lands, and see the wondrous things he had brought therefrom.

One relic, and one only, of that voyage Bristol still retains—the famous "rib of the Dun Cow" (cow-whale) preserved with religious care in Redcliffe Church; the

Rib of the Whale in St. Mary Redcliffe Church.

covered in recent times among the City records. "1497—Item. Paid for settynge upp ye bone of ye bigge fyshe and ... (writing illegible) hys worke brote over seas, *vid.* For two rings of iron iiijd."

According to Socino, who wrote on Dec. 18th of this same year, Cabot recorded his discoveries on a map and also on a globe; but no trace of either has been found, although La Cosa must have had access to them for his map.

In the following year, 1498, the King granted a supplementary charter in the name of John Cabot only, authorising him to take out six ships to the "lande and isles of late founde by the said John," at his own cost, to trade and colonize; giving him for the latter purpose "300 prisoners"—doubtless glad enough to be rid of them, the gaols being full to overflowing just then in consequence of Perkin Warbeck's rebellion. Bounties were also allowed to "James Carter, Thos. Bradley, and Lancelot Thirkill, of Bristowe," for fitting out three of the ships.

The expedition sailed, made further discoveries, and returned; but whether it was under the control of John Cabot is not known, for here all record of the elder Cabot ceases.

Sebastian says his father died about this time, but he gives neither date or place of burial. It seems most probable that John Cabot's death occurred at

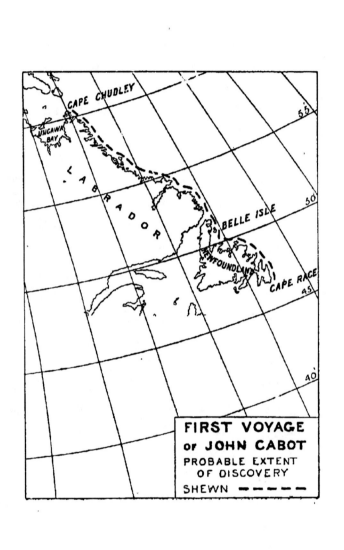

FIRST VOYAGE
of JOHN CABOT
PROBABLE EXTENT
OF DISCOVERY

SHEWN — — — —

contested—accompanied him on this voyage, returned in command. Strangely enough, no account of the expedition appears to exist among English records; the sole fact of its return being gathered from the presence in London of Lancelot Thirkill, June 6, 1501, and his repayment of the loan he had had of the King. From foreign sources, however, we know that it was John Cabot's intention in this expedition to follow the shore from his former discovery till he reached the equinoctial regions; and we also know that (whether under his command or that of Sebastian) the plan was pursued until lack of provisions compelled its abandonment.

The second expedition, taking a more northerly course than the first, visited Iceland, and then steering west, made the coast of Labrador, named by Cabot "De la Terra de los Baccalaos," "The Land of the Cod-fish," from the immense shoals of those fish which they encountered. Landing the colonists, though whereabouts in that inhospitable region is not stated, they sailed still farther to the north-west — through Hudson's Straits — until "affrighted by the monstrous heaps of ice swimming in the sea, and the continual daylight," they dared go no further.

Retracing their course they found many of the colonists dead of cold and hunger and re-embarking

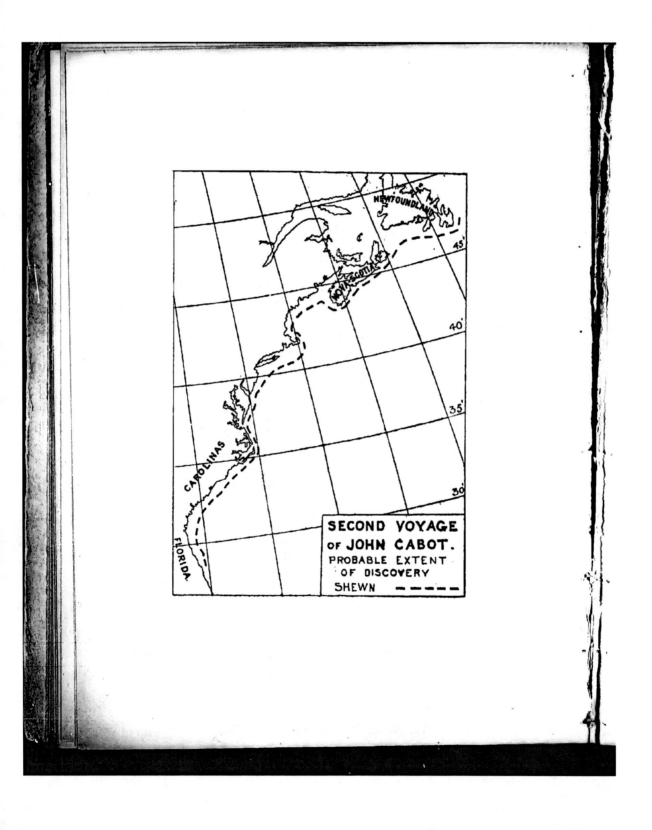

SECOND VOYAGE
of JOHN CABOT.
PROBABLE EXTENT
OF DISCOVERY
SHEWN   - - - - -

who had freighted the vessels deemed, for they had not found the golden goal of Cathay nor even established a trading colony! But in reality successful beyond the wildest dreams of King or people, for there is no doubt that the Cabot charter and the voyages made pursuant to it, were always regarded as the root of England's title to her American possessions, and that, "to the daring and genius of Cabot is owing the occupation of the northern continent by an English-speaking race, with their vast energies and wealth. But for the Cabots Spain might have monopolized discovery in North as well as in South America."

Eschewing the "trade of merchandise," Sebastian Cabot appears to have devoted himself entirely to nautical science; attaining such eminence that, on the death of Columbus, the King of Spain engaged his services as Cartographer, at a salary of 30,000 maravedas, intending to send him on another voyage. Before the design could be carried out, Ferdinand died, and Sebastian returned to England.

Under the auspices of Henry VIII., he is said to have again crossed the Atlantic seeking a passage the variations of the magnetic needle, Cabot returned.

A few years later he was again in the service of Spain, engaged under the young Emperor, Charles V., as Pilot-major, at a largely increased salary. This post he retained during the greater part of Charles' reign. It was while holding it that he made to Contarini those dishonest offers of information ... ' those misleading statements concerning his which have proved so prolific in controversy to his biographers.

In 1526, Cabot commanded a Spanish expedition to Brazil, which although he penetrated some distance into the interior, ended disastrously, and resulted in his being imprisoned for a year on the charge of " mismanagement and excesses."

The first count of the indictment may have been true. Very probably the great cartographer was not skilled in the management of men. As Oviedo, the Spanish historian, sapiently remarked, " it is not the same thing to command and govern people as to point a quadrant or an astrolabe " ; but the " excesses " charged against him were far more likely to have been committed by the Portugese, who had sent out a rival expedition, and to whose malicious intrigues and jealous interference the disasters of the Spaniards were mainly due. Untruthful and covetous of honours and gold, Sebastian has been proved ; but that he was also kindly, gentle, and humane, there is no

While in the employ of Spain, Cabot made his "Mappamundi," or Map of the World. This famous map, which not only presented his own and his father's discoveries, but those of Spain and Portugal down to his own time, was drawn on parchment and illuminated with gold and colours. The original was sold on the death of the President of the Council of the Indies in 1575, and has never since been heard of. Several engravings of it were made, only one of which is now known; that in the Galerie de Géographie, Paris.

Soon after Henry VIII. death, the Council of the young King, Edward, induced Cabot to return to England, and, according to Strype, he settled in Bristol, 1548.

Charles V., through his ambassador, commanded his return; but the Privy Council replied that "he refused to go either into Spain or to the Emperor, and that, being of that mind, *and the King's subject*, no reason or equity would that he should be forced against his will."

Charles immediately stopped his pension, but

maritime affairs of the Kingdom, and adding to his store of charts and "discourses."

In 1551, a general stagnation of trade pervaded England, and the London merchants consulted Cabot, who had just succeeded in breaking the monopoly of the German "Merchants of the Steelyard," as to what steps could be taken to revive it. Through his

Hall of the Merchant Venturers' Society, Bristol.

advice they formed themselves into the "Company of Merchant Adventurers of London" (of which the Bristol "Merchant Venturers" is an outcome) for the search and discovery of the northern part of the world by sea, and to open a way and passage to Cathay by the north-east.

Cabot, in recognition of his services, was made Governor for life, and immediately set about building

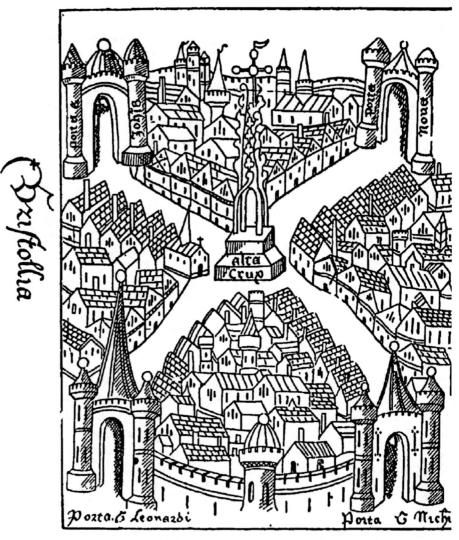

Plan of Ancient Bristol.

Great was the rejoicing when the first expedit
put to sea, May 20th, 1553. The ships were tov
down the Thames by boats, "and being come n

to Greenwich, where the Court then lay, the courtiers came running out, and the common people flocked together upon the shores in crowdes ; the Privy Council they lookt out of the windowes of the Court, and the rest ranne up to the toppes of the towers," while the "skies rang agayne with the shouts of the mariners and the firing of the shippe's ordnance." But, alas ! the young king who would have taken so keen an interest in the show, being well learned in all matters pertaining to the sea, was lying sick unto death in his room in the Palace, and e'er the ships were well on their way he had breathed his last.

The expedition, and others that followed, succeeded in opening up Russia and extending English trade across the Caspian Sea into Central Asia—to the jubilant delight of the organiser of them ! Stephen Boroughs, who commanded the last of these expeditions (a little pinnace called the " Swiftsure ") gives the following quaint picture of the Ancient Mariner, who came aboard the pinnace to see them off :—

" The goode olde gentleman, Master Cabota, gave to the poore most liberall almes, wishing them to praye for the good fortune and prosperous successe of the ' Serchthrift,' our pinnesse. And then, at the sign of the Christopher, he and his friends banketted, and made me and them that were in the companie great cheere ; and, for very joy that he had to see the towardness of our intended discovery, he enter'd into governance of Almighty God."

This is the last public appearance of Cabot of which we have any record. How long he lived, or where he died, is not known, and can only be inferred from the facts that his pension ceased to be drawn after 1557, and that Eden, who lived in London, was present at his deathbed.

The only literary relics of Cabot known to exist are the engraved map of 1544 and its facsimile. Of his other "remains," voluminous though they must have been, there is no trace. Hakluyt, writing of Cabot in 1582, says, "Shortly shall come out in print all his own mappes and discourses drawne and written by himselfe, which are in the custody of the Worshipful Master William Worthington." The publication was never made, and no one knows what has become of them. It is, however, strongly suspected that they found their way to Spain, through the instrumentality of the said "Master Worthington" (Cabot's associate in office), who seems to have been but indifferent honest. If .'.' were so, there is hope that they are still in existe. and may some day be restored.

One relic we had of Cabot—the famous portrait, painted when he was an old man, and which in 1625

Effigies Sebastiani Caboti Angli
Filii Johanis Caboti Vene
Ti Militis Avrati Primi
Invet Oris Terræ Novasvb
Herico VII. Angl. Iæ Rege.

hung in the King's gallery at Whitehall. In 1792, this picture was presented to Charles J. Harford, Esquire, of Bristol, who discovered it while in Scotland; but, unfortunately for Bristolians, he sold it to Mr. John Biddle of Pittsburg, and it perished in the destruction of that gentleman's house by fire in 1848. Several copies exist in America, and an excellent engraving of the picture was made by Rawle of Bristol. Cabot is represented in his robe and chain as Governor of the Merchant Adventurers. There is also a painting of John Cabot and his three sons in the Ducal Palace, Venice.

Although the maps and charts of the Cabots are so far, lost to us whom they most concern, clear traces of them exist in the work of foreign cosmographers, and especially in the famous map of Juan de la Cosa, published in 1501, only three years after the voyage of John Cabot; where the row of British flags, commencing at the southern end with *Mar descubierta por inglese*, "sea discovered by the English;" and ending at the north with *Cavo de ynglaterra*, "Cape of England," mark unmistakably the discoveries of Cabot, and could have been obtained only from his map.

The most curious evidence, however, comes from

In the British Museum is a facsimile, by Wm. Griggs, of the original "Carta Universal," or Chart of the World, preserved in the "Propaganda" at Rome, by which Pope Alexander VI. divided the unclaimed lands of the globe between Spain and Portugal. On this unique chart the Northern Continent ends at Labrador, which is described as a country "which was discovered by the English of the town of Bristol, and which is of no use !"

Truly,

> "When a thing's beyond our power,
> We say in scorn, '*the grapes are sour* !'"

St. Augustine's Gateway

Brandon Hill, Bristol,
The Site of the Cabot Memorial.

———

Brandon Hill, the site of Bristol's memorial to th[e] Cabots, lies between the north-west portion of th[e] city and the wooded heights of Clifton.

A fringe of houses encircles the base, but th[e] remainder of its twenty-five acres, up to the round[e] summit, 250 feet high, is open greensward, wi[t] gravelled paths, and seats under shady hawthor[n] bushes—the happy haunt of children from all parts of the city ; and, as evening spreads her dusky mantle around, of whispering lovers, every seat accommodating a pair, sometimes two!

The Hill takes its name from the Irish saint, Brendan, a chapel and hermitage dedicated to him having once stood on its summit.

This St. Brendan is said to have been a great sailor,

The Cross

discovered land across the Atlantic. Whether the claim be true or false, certain it is that the story of his "voyages," and the golden legends connected therewith, aroused men's curiosity and incited to subsequent expeditions, which, nearly a thousand years after Brendan's death, resulted in the discovery of the Northern Continent. The choice, therefore, of "St. Brendon's Hill" for the site of the memorial

of that discovery is peculiarly appropriate; more especially as Brendan was the patron saint of sailors, and his chapel much frequented by Bristol mariners.

The first known occupant of the hermitage, in 1351, was "Lucy de Newchurch," who, tired of the world, begged permission to immure herself therein. Fifty years later it was tenanted by a hermit, Reginald Taylor. Bluff King Hal, however, made short work of both chapel and hermitage, and in the troubled times of the Civil War a fort took their place, traces of which still remain. It is upon the site of this fort, recently occupied by two Russian cannon, that the memorial tower will stand. In digging out the foundations was discovered, beneath the soft concrete of the chapel, a grave containing human bones, which, in all probability, are those of the ancient denizens of the spot!

No finer view of Bristol and its environs can  be obtained anywhere than from the Hill. On the right rise the woods and mansions of Clifton, and its Parish Church, "severely simple!" In the valley between is Jacobs Wells, the old Jewish quarter. The City schools were built on the ancient burial ground, which gave rise to the witty if gruesome remark that, "whatever the boys might lack they were always sure of a good Hebrew foundation." Thanks to Queen Elizabeth, the boys' mothers have been always sure of a good "drying ground!" Her Majesty having secured to them for purposes; in recognition, it is said, of the faultless style in which their progenitors "got up" the immense ruffles worn by herself when visiting the City. Immediately on the left is St. Michael's Hill, the site of another large fort; and Tyndall's Park and mansion, still possessed by a branch of the family whence sprang William Tyndall, the translator of the Bible, the only perfect copy of whose first edition is still preserved in the Baptist College hard by. Beyond, and spreading for miles along the valley, bounded on its opposite side by Bedminster Downs and Dundry Hill, lies the City with its churches and schools, its ancient buildings (now, alas! rapidly disappearing), its modern warehouses and factories, its venerable cathedral and historic "green," encircled by avenues of limes. And, intersecting its southern side, the floating harbour, formed by the Avon and Frome, and bearing on its capacious bosom the merchandise of many lands, carried in craft of all sizes, from the tiny coasting lugger to the huge, perfectly equipped Atlantic steamer.

And not a ship among them all, going or coming, but must pass within full view of Brandon Hill, whose long southern slope stretches to within a few hundred yards of the water's edge!

CPSIA information can be obtained at www.ICGtesting.com
Printed in the USA
BVOW03s1512190814

363415BV00023B/969/P